BULLYING

By
Holly Duhig

BookLife
PUBLISHING

©2018
**BookLife Publishing
King's Lynn
Norfolk PE30 4LS**

All rights reserved.
Printed in Malaysia.

A catalogue record for this book is
available from the British Library.

ISBN: 978-1-78637-398-4

Written by:
Holly Duhig

Edited by:
Kirsty Holmes

Designed by:
Amy Li

All facts, statistics, web addresses
and URLs in this book were verified
as valid and accurate at time of
writing. No responsibility for any
changes to external websites or
references can be accepted by
either the author or publisher.

PHOTO CREDITS

BULLYING

Words that look like **this** can be found in the glossary on page 24.

What Is Bullying?

People upset other people **accidentally** all the time. Usually, we say sorry to each other and feel better. Bullying is not like this. It is done on purpose.

"I'm sorry!"

"That's OK."

Bullying is a way of behaving that hurts other people, with words or actions, more than once. It can make people feel very sad.

How Bullying Happens

Bullying can hurt people **physically**. Actions that hurt other people, such as pushing and shoving, are a type of bullying.

Tripping

Hitting

Breaking People's Belongings

Name Calling

Leaving People Out

Starting Rumours

Teasing

Bullying can also hurt people **emotionally**. Name calling and leaving people out on purpose can hurt people's feelings and is a form of bullying.

Why Bullying Happens

People often bully to make others feel bad, and make themselves feel better. If someone is jealous of you, they might try to make you feel bad about yourself.

Sometimes bullies have been bullied themselves. Someone might have made them feel **inferior**. By putting other people down, they can make themselves feel more powerful.

There are lots of reasons people bully, but there's never an excuse.

Who Can Bully?

People often think that bullies are always big and tough, but this is not true. Anyone can behave in a bullying way. Bullies are not always strangers. Often, bullies are your friends.

Who is being bullied in this picture?

Both boys and girls can behave in a bullying way. Sometimes, adults can bully others too. Often, people bully when they feel **insecure**.

Self-Confidence

People often pick on someone who is different in some way. This is usually because the bullies don't want people to notice what's different about them. Being different is a good thing.

If everyone was the same, the world would be very boring.

Having self-confidence is about loving what makes you different. Bullying is about trying to make people feel bad, so your self-confidence is like your **armour.**

"I used to get picked on for my curly hair. The bullying stopped when I told them that I love my hair just the way it is."

Maya – aged 7

You Might Feel Embarrassed

Embarrassing someone in front of others is a type of bullying. This is not OK. People usually do this because they are **ashamed** about something in their own lives.

Scarlet – aged 6

"My friends would always try to trip me up.

My teacher told me that real friends don't embarass

each other, and they are the ones who should feel ashamed."

If someone is scared of being bullied, they might try to make someone else the centre of attention by embarrassing them. **15**

You Might Feel Scared

Threatening someone is another type of bullying behaviour. This can make you feel very scared. People threaten others because making someone else feel scared makes them feel more powerful.

Headache

Beating Heart

There are lots of ways our bodies react to feeling scared.

Sick Stomach

Sweating Hands

No-one should have to feel scared of anyone else. Always tell an adult if you are being bullied, so that they can help you.

"Going to school made me feel sick so I had to stay home. I soon realised I wasn't sick. I was just scared of the bullying at school."

Eliza – aged 7

You Might Feel Angry

If you are being bullied, it's normal to feel angry. You might want to hit or shout at the person who is bullying you. It's important never to hurt someone, though.

People who bully like getting a **reaction**.

Shouting and hitting might make the bullying worse.

Anton – aged 8

"Being bullied made me feel like a weakling. I know it's wrong, but picking on someone else made me feel strong again."

Often, people bully because they have been bullied themselves in the past. When people feel angry about being bullied, they might take their anger out on somebody else. This is never OK.

19

What to Do If You Are Being Bullied

If you are being bullied, it's OK to stand up for yourself. If someone is saying mean things to you, it's OK to tell them that they're wrong, or to leave you alone.

Standing up for yourself is a good thing,

but hurting people is never OK.

Always tell an adult if you're being bullied. You can tell a parent, carer, a teacher or even a school nurse.

"I was scared to tell my teacher I was being bullied because I thought she wouldn't believe me, but she did believe me and she helped a lot."

Imran – aged 7

What to Do If Someone You Know Is Being Bullied

Sometimes you will see other people getting bullied. It is important to speak up and let someone know if you see this happening.

"Ryan was new to our school and was being bullied because of his accent. I was worried about sticking up for him but I did it anyway. Now Ryan is my best friend."

Caleb – aged 6

If you see someone who is being left out on purpose, try to make friends with them. If your friends are bullying someone, let them know that this is not OK.

GLOSSARY

accidentally	without meaning to; not on purpose
armour	metal coverings worn to protect the body
ashamed	feeling embarrassed or guilty
emotionally	in a way that relates to one's feelings
inferior	worse in quality or lower in status
insecure	lacking in self-confidence
physically	in a way that relates to the body
reaction	an action or response to something that has been done
threatening	to say that you will harm someone or do something unpleasant

INDEX